Guide &

Your Pet Dog's ᴮᵉⁿᵃ

David Ryan PG Dip (CABC), CCAB

ISBN 978-1-291-94611-6

Guide & Control
Your Pet Dog's Behaviour

David Ryan PG Dip (CABC), CCAB

Contents

The author

I have a confession to make. I am still learning about dog behaviour. In fact, the more I learn about the behaviour of the domestic dog, the more I think there is to find out.

I was a police dog handler and instructor for twenty six years, handling and instructing others in handling dogs from fifty kilo German Shepherds down to five kilo working Cockers. They taught me a lot about hands-on practice.

Towards the end of that time I passed Southampton University's post graduate diploma in Companion Animal Behaviour Counselling, with distinction. That taught me a lot about the theory and how it applies in practice.

I joined the Association of Pet Behaviour Counsellors, and served as Chairman for three years, before stepping down in 2012, and spent ten years helping owners with pet behaviour problems. That taught me a lot about how people relate to their pets.

I was granted certification as a Clinical Animal Behaviourist by the Association for the Study of Animal Behaviour in 2008 and have had the privilege of discussing dogs with some of the world's best behaviourists. They continue to teach me about the cutting edge of dog behaviour.

Amongst others, I've worked with and for the Animal Behaviour and Training Council, the RSPCA at national and local level, and the PDSA. I lecture on Newcastle University's MSc in Applied Animal Behaviour and Welfare, and on Police Dog Legislation Officer courses, which teach me some different viewpoints.

I continue to help local and national charities with dog assessment and re-homing to keep me on my toes, but mostly because every dog I meet teaches me something.

The common theme I've found across all the different aspects of dog ownership is that problems occur when the dog/owner relationship is out of kilter. Balancing that relationship is not only a vital part of improving pet behaviour, but also improves the quality of life for all pets and owners.

This booklet is about harmonising that relationship and using it to control pets by communicating and interacting with them in ways that they understand. If I was trendier I would call it "lifestyle" or "holistic", but I prefer to think of it as simply guiding the behaviour of dogs by controlling what's important to them.

Meet Finlay

Finlay is a six month old Cocker-poo owned by David's brother, Colin. His Mum was a working cocker spaniel and his Dad was a miniature poodle (Finlay's, not Colin's).

Colin adopted him when his owners found him "too lively" and tried to return him to his breeder, who wouldn't have him back.

He was supposed to model for Colin's pen pictures, but often didn't sit still for long enough. On the other hand he doesn't actually behave as badly as some of our concocted illustrations suggest.

Finlay is a typical young Cocker-poo who believes that everybody is his friend and that life is for throwing yourself headlong into. He's not yet perfectly behaved, but he's getting there.

Colin and his son Max take Finlay for long walks in the country and by the seaside to tire him out. They have not yet succeeded.

Guide & Control

Many problem behaviours are caused or aggravated by a breakdown in the harmony between pet and owner, and lots of owners find it difficult to relate to their dogs in ways that allow them to control their pet's behaviour.

All dogs need to be controlled - apart from anything else, the law requires it - but often trying to enforce your will by confronting a dog can provoke a worse reaction and either escalate a problem or change the nature of it.

Rather than attempting to dominate a pet oppressively, or trying to apply pack dynamics in what is essentially a family situation, pets need guidance in good manners from their owners.

Resource-control as a way of changing pet dogs' behaviour has been around in various forms for some time, and a refreshed interpretation, taking account of modern dog training methods, is the most efficient and effective way to start or restructure a relationship.

Guide & Control can and should be used as a basis for owners' relationships with puppies right from the start, for dogs with behavioural issues, and particularly for quickly establishing new relationships with dogs adopted as adults. We can establish control by providing guidance, without confrontation.

The principle is simplicity itself, and based on tried and tested learning theory. We all know what a good job guide dogs for the blind and other assistance dogs do for people. They work by providing guidance for their handlers and so prevent them getting into difficulties. They guide before problems occur.

Each time they encounter an obstacle that might cause their handler a problem they guide them in the right direction. They step sideways around the lamppost. What they don't do is to wait until their handler splats into the lamppost, then tell them off for being wrong.

7

They don't allow the person for whom they are responsible to walk into the path of a bus because they see the bus coming and take preventative action.

Why do we think it is a good idea to wait until our dog does something wrong, then try to explain why it is wrong and what he should have done instead? Or, even worse, just tell him off without telling him what he should have done? How would you like to live your life like that?

There is a deep and meaningful relationship between guide dogs and their handlers based on mutual trust, because the dog takes care of the handler.

Turn that around and we can take care of our pet dogs in the same way; by providing guidance *before* they fall into problem behaviours. The first part of that guidance is learning how to live in harmony in their own family - the good social manners we all need.

Resources

The underpinning philosophy of Guide & Control is that by controlling the resources that are important to your dog you can guide him to the kind of behaviour that is appropriate in the circumstances.

You also become a person of immense value, to whom your dog looks for all the good things in life; the person who is listened to because your guidance is valued by your dog. Control of these resources gives you control over your dog because he wants to do what you want him to do. This gives you the ability to guide your dog into the right behaviour before he makes a mistake.

Put simply:

> Your dog likes stuff.
>
> You have the stuff your dog likes.
>
> Because he likes the stuff, he will do as you ask to get some stuff.
>
> Control the stuff and you control the dog.
>
> Control the dog and you can guide him into good behaviour.
>
> Guide him to the behaviour that gets him stuff and you are his god.

So, what is this stuff? What are these magic resources? Well, the simple answer is, "anything your dog wants", but the complication is that each dog is different, so their value of resources will be different too. However, for simplicity we can categorise them under three headings: Food, Activities and Interaction, although we might find some overlap.

Food

Food is the easiest to describe, so we'll start with that. But I should point out that if your dog is showing *any* signs of aggression around food, do NOT go any further with this. You need specialist help. Guide & Control will be part of the programme of change, but it needs to be structured with other aspects that will serve your individual case.

Taking control of food is relatively simple for humans because we have an opposable thumb and can use a tin-opener (not to mention the ability to push a wonky-wheeled supermarket trolley).

When we feed our dogs is also our choice, and this is crucial, not in terms of the actual time of day, or even in relation to what our dog is doing at the time, but in what behaviour our dog *thinks* results in us giving them the food.

Dogs are very good at associative learning; they quickly learn that one thing follows another. They learn *very* quickly when something they do is followed by a consequence. But it is *their* perception of how they achieved that consequence that has most bearing on their tendency to behave like that again. It's what's in their head that counts.

If 'X' is a result Finlay wants and he thinks that doing 'Y' gets him it, he will repeat Y when he wants X, even if it was only a coincidence the first time! If he thinks Y gets him X, but Y *doesn't* work this time, he will try more Y, becoming even Y-ier; taking it up a notch to extra-Y or Y-plus.

If you are slow with the tin-opener and through frustration or excitement your dog gives out a little woof just before you place her bowl on the floor, she may well think that "*woof*" gets her the food. Now, we know it was just a coincidence, but her perception was different. She now thinks that when she woofs, you put the food down; that *she* made *you* put the food down on the floor for her; that *she* controls her access to the food.

Next mealtime she knows what to do when she is hungry - she woofs at you to tell you to put the food down. And you do because you were going to anyway. But from her perspective, she told you what to do, and you did it. Who do you think is guiding who here? Who is in control?

This one small interaction starts to give her the impression that you do as you are told. And if you do as you are told over an important resource like food, what else will you do when she tells you?

Remember, it is the importance of the resource to her, not to you, that counts. We know it doesn't matter much to you when you put her food down, but this is an important event for her.

So, what *should* you do? You are developing the family manners of puppies and of dogs that are new to the household, so you need to establish polite behaviour from the start. Make up her meal in her bowl and take it, and her, to an appropriate place to feed her. It is a good idea to make this place identifiable with a bed, fleece or mat, so she knows this is the place to go to be fed. Using her bed also makes training her to go to her bed easier - a double incentive!

When you get there (she'll follow you because you have a food bowl in your hand), manipulate the bowl above her head so that she walks onto the bed, then say, "Sit" as you lift it over her head - the same as teaching a sit with a treat.

As her bum hits the bed take the food-bowl to the floor in front of her. If she does anything other than stay sitting calmly (stands, jumps up, woofs or dives in to the bowl), lift the bowl up a little to indicate that she has done the wrong thing. If she stays sitting, the food comes closer; anything else, the food moves away.

Don't tell her off - we're guiding her, not chastising her. You are communicating with her through the movement of the food-bowl, so you don't need to talk at all - speech just gets in the way.

You might need to do this a couple of times before she gets the idea that moving doesn't get her the food. Don't repeat the word "Sit" as she already knows what you've asked, but you can use the bowl to lure her into place again if you need to.

Because she moves quickly, you'll need to be quick too. Bum on bed - bowl goes down; bum lifts - bowl rises. Really fast responses from you help her to understand that it is her actions that have the consequences, and she will learn quicker.

This isn't a tease or a test, so get the bowl on the floor as soon as she sits. Keep hold of it (thanking our monkey ancestors for that opposable thumb) and be prepared to move it again. You will probably only need small movements once she realises what they mean.

When she sits still for half a second with the bowl on the floor, remove your hand and tell her, "*Take it*". Then stand up, tell her what a good dog she has been, and leave her alone whilst she eats.

You are controlling the food bowl, and therefore her access to an important resource, conditional on her behaviour. Sitting quietly gets her the food, anything else delays it. Good manners are rewarded, but inappropriate behaviours aren't. You guide her behaviour by controlling the food.

You can improve each successive time by waiting for more calmness, slightly longer, or for her to look at you. She will look at you naturally when you move the bowl away or delay your "Take it" signal, because she realises she needs guidance in how to behave, and that you hold the key. The look means, "*What shall I do?*" and rewarding it with "*Take it*" reinforces it as a desired behaviour. In this way she learns that sitting calmly and looking at you is an appropriate way of asking, "*Please may I start to eat now?*"

Don't ever be tempted to take her food away once you have told her she can take it. Once you have given it to her, it is hers; she owns it and is entitled to it. Taking it from her again only makes you mean and nasty, and her suspicious and defensive. How would you like it if I invited you round for a meal and, whilst you were tucking in, whipped the plate out from in front of you, "just to show you who's boss"?

For dogs that have already fallen into bad habits, for example leaping about or barking excitedly (but NOT for aggression unless a qualified behaviourist has advised you to), you can use the same process, but you will need to teach him the new behaviour out of context first.

The fabulously named Yerkes-Dodson Law[1] shows us that when his levels of arousal are too high (mealtimes), his ability to perform reduces; he's too excited to learn the new behaviour properly.

The solution is to train a "sit-on-bed" when it isn't mealtime, so that when you ask for it in context he understands what you mean. That way you don't need to get into a, "Don't do that!" argument, you just need to guide him by showing him what to do to get his food. The movement of the bowl in your hand says, "Do this" and, when he does, the food appears. If you need help with training the "sit-on-bed", check out the Training Guide at the end of this booklet.

This is great for scheduled meals, but what about tit-bits? You know, those little bits of digestive biscuit or corner-of-sandwich that we share? The same reasoning applies - what does your dog think gained him the snack? Was he jumping up and down and pawing at you? Or was he lying quietly near your feet? Whatever he thinks got him the treat is what he will be more likely to do the next time. Is he *telling* you to treat him? What does he think?

The choice of which behaviour to reward with the treat is yours. The best thing to do would be to simply wait to share until your dog voluntarily performs a behaviour you like. Pop the morsel into your pocket or into his food-bowl on the shelf until then (see under "Treats" in the Training Guide).

If you are pressed for time or can't wait for any other reason (laziness is *not* a good reason), the second best course of action would be to engineer an appropriate behaviour. Maybe ask your dog to go lie down for a few moments and, when he's relaxed, reward that calmness with the biscuit-crumb.

---

[1] Named after psychologists Robert Mearns Yerkes and John Dillingham Dodson in 1908 after their publication "*The relation of strength of stimulus to rapidity of habit-formation*" in the Journal of Comparative Neurology and Psychology 18: 459–482. "Yerkes" pronounced "y uh r - k ee z". Now you can impress your friends!

You are looking for behaviours that are calm and encourage relaxation, not ones that excite him and build up frustration if not quickly rewarded. Behaviours you can extend, rather than short behaviours; ones that teach him self-control.

Pawing, or even raising a paw, isn't a great choice as it is over in a flash, so he'll repeat it, and again and again and again... increasing his frustration because he has done the thing and his reward hasn't arrived. Neither is it good to keep changing behaviours so that he has to guess which one

you want this time. This trains dogs that paw, then other paw, then both paws, then sit, then sit-up-and-beg, then bark, then spin, then... frantically trying all sorts of things for half a second and winding themselves up into a frenzy of frustration.

Make sure that there's a good break between any inappropriate behaviour and the preferred one, so that he doesn't get the idea that he can make you give him the treat by behaving badly, so you have to tell him to behave, then you reward him.

It's called "chaining" behaviours, where one leads to another and eventually the reward, and it is something else that dogs are very good at. In this scenario he would behave badly, guiding you into telling him how to be good, which ends in a reward for him. He would think behaving badly was the key to getting what he wants from you.

Now, don't get the idea that that you can't share with your pet if you want to, because nothing could be further from the truth. In short, share when he's behaving well and, if he's not, simply either wait until later, when he is, or guide a better behaviour and share (after a break to prevent chaining).

That way he follows your guidance into good behaviour to get the very reward you were going to give him anyway. Treats arrive when he's on his best behaviour.

So the old maxim of, *"he must do something for you before you do something for him"* was half right. Think of it more as, *"he must be behaving appropriately when you do something for him."*

When he gets the idea that calmness is involved, that alone will suffice, and you can then turn the training on its head. So long as he isn't doing anything inappropriate, you can reward him. Life becomes so much easier. He starts to be calm because calm behaviour is often rewarded, and because he is calm you can reward him any time; a lovely virtuous circle.

The same principles apply to all the other resources he values.

Activities

For an activity to be a resource it has to have value in itself or be a precursor to something else that has value, so things like: having his lead clipped on (to go out), going through the door (to the garden), having the ball thrown or a tug on a rope-toy, getting into the car (to go somewhere), getting out of the car (to go somewhere), having his lead clipped off (to be free!), playing with the dogs in the park, holding a ball in her mouth (for retrievers), staring at the ball (for collies), chasing the ball, or any other activity that his breed was originally intended to do (running under/behind a carriage for Dalmatians) … basically any of the things your dog enjoys.

Essentially, if it is something he likes to do, or leads to something he likes to do, it is an activity-resource. There are loads of them.

Because he enjoys these activities he will "work" - be prepared to pay a small cost - in order to indulge in them. He will also try to gain access to them. The more important they are to him, the more effort he will put into doing that. But we have to bear in mind that their value can change over time.

We all realise that the value of food depends upon both how yummy we personally find it and how hungry we are. When you are starving you'll find a dry crust more valuable than the nicest treat when you are stuffed full.

The same "personal value" plus "deprivation value" applies to activities. A Frisbee throw may have more personal value for a collie than for a bloodhound (although not necessarily depending upon the individual). The sixty-fifth Frisbee throw is probably less valuable than the first, even for the collie (although not necessarily ...). So we are always walking a tightrope, balancing preferences for activities.

That said, we aren't necessarily going to ask our pets for a huge down-payment to indulge in their activities - just some appropriate behaviour. To gain access to the garden for a wander about just needs a bit of calm; anything he can recognise as being, "the-way-I-ask-to-go-out".

You can choose the way he asks to go out because he can't open the door and you can. You can either accept his metaphorically yelling, "*OPEN-THE-DOOR-OPEN-THE-DOOR-OPEN-THE-DOOR!!*" at you, or you could shape, "*Please could you open the door for me?*" And therein lies the crux of controlling activities. It should be him asking politely, not demanding or telling you.

Again, as with the food, you will be looking to reward calm behaviour. Standing still is okay, but it can sometimes be difficult to explain to him that it is the standing still that gets the door open; after all, he was probably going to stand there anyway.

You are looking for something he can actively do that is calm and paying you attention. Something he can use to ask you if he can go out now, please. After all, it is only good manners. So, calmly sitting and looking at you is probably what you are after. What a coincidence!

You can train this in the same way that you trained good manners for food, except you have more opportunities. Take your dog to the door. If she wants to go out anyway, her reward will be you opening the door. If she doesn't want to go out, you can increase her  incentive by letting her see you put something attractive outside (tiny food treat, a favourite toy, or maybe a husband).

Say, "*Sit*", just once. Place your hand on the door handle and wait. Wait until she sits, and then wait until she looks at you. If she doesn't sit, fold your arms - the equivalent of moving the food bowl away. When she does, tell her how pleased you are and open the door with a small fanfare, or at least a flourish and a, "*Go on*".

Whilst she is learning, reward what you can. "Shaping" behaviour is working towards the ultimate goal by accepting and rewarding the least little part of it to start with, whilst improving it at each successive attempt. The slightest bump of the bum on the floor might be enough for the very first time.

At this stage calmness is a bonus, but eventually you will need to factor that in too. If she is too on-edge to be calm (Yerkes-Dodson!), then next time you can reduce the incentive to go out (ordinary kibble, least favourite toy, ex-boyfriend?) and reward her sitting with long languid strokes of your hand gently down the back of her neck.

Now control the opening of the door so that she remains sitting until asked to, "*Go on*". Open it a tiny crack. If she stays sitting tell her she's good. If she doesn't, close it again until she sits. Keep opening it progressively further until she gets the idea that if she sits, the door opens, but if she gets up before asked, it closes.

Stretch out the calm-sitting for a couple of seconds whilst the door opens and reduce the flourishing a bit as you let her out, and you have the makings of a dog that sits and looks at you calmly every time you and her approach a door. This is a far more effective way of controlling her than the old "resource-control" of wrestling with her so you could get through the door first.

Toys and games are special forms of activity because whilst most activities are under your control as default - you just need to ensure the behaviour she provides to ask for them is appropriate - she can actually control toys and some games she plays with you. Games together are also a form of Interaction with you (see later) so they are a double-whammy of a reward.

For that reason we split toys/games into two kinds: self-play toys/games and interactive toys/games (although there is some cross-over). As the name suggests, self-play is when your dog plays with a toy by herself, and this is something we want to encourage to give her access to fun things that aren't utterly dependent upon us.

All dogs should have access to toys if they want them, and most dogs do. You will notice that your dog has preferences for types of toy and you will probably want to buy ones that your dog enjoys playing with. Don't be misled into thinking, as one of my clients did, that her dog hated tennis balls because he always destroyed them. That actually means he loves tennis balls, but you need to get him quite a robust version to chew on.

Rather than allowing your dog to leave his toys lying around the house for you to pick up, provide him with a toy-box to keep them in (cardboard or luxury oak with the words "BENJI'S TOYS" engraved upon it - you choose). Teach him to put them back when he's finished with them (it's a retrieve with you standing the other side of the box and a "drop" at the right time).

The toys being in the box isn't just tidy, it also means that access to them is slightly restricted, so when your dog finds one at the bottom that he hasn't played with for a while, it is a little more attractive than it otherwise would have been. Like strutting out in that that jacket you found at the back of your wardrobe - you haven't worn it or a while, but actually you like it more than you remember.

"*Go get a toy*" is also a good alternative behaviour to many inappropriate ones - a good behaviour to guide at crucial times. "*Put your toys away*" is a great interactive game too.

"Interactive" toys and games are those that she plays with you. As I said, these bestride activities and interactions and so are doubly important. You must make sure that she knows that these are *your* games in which she is invited to take part, because both toys and you belong to you, not to her.

Retain possession of interactive toys yourself - don't leave them lying about like a self-play toy. Restricting access to them to play-times with you gives them immense value as a reward.

Of course this means you should keep them at the end of the game and that she has to give them up when asked. You don't always have to win during the game because that's no fun, but you must make sure that her behaviour is appropriate and that she gives your toy back again. There's a training guide for games at the end of the booklet.

In order to initiate a game, your dog must ask appropriately. "Sit and look"?

I knew a police dog whose handler once rewarded him for spinning by throwing a ball. Just once. After that, he would spin in a circle when he wanted the ball thrown (which was a lot) and if it didn't work he would spin again, and again... We managed to change it back to "sit and look", but it was poor guidance in the first place that gave the dog the wrong impression.

So, for repeated throws in a fetch-game your dog must bring the toy back and give it up each time, then wait without an inappropriate behaviour for the next throw. And the same for tug-games; let go when asked and wait for the next offer to tug. Unfortunately, explaining to a dog, "don't do anything inappropriate" is a much harder concept than, "do this for your reward", so teach a well-mannered behaviour, like sit and look. Shape it by controlling the resource - the same as the food-bowl and door training (see Training Guide).

Just before your dog has had enough interactive play, quietly say, "*Finished*" and put the toy away in your pocket, or on the shelf. This way you control the end of the game and also leave your dog wanting to please you just a little bit more.

People ask, "*Can I play tug? I heard it was a bad thing?*" Playing tug is fine so long as you are in ultimate control; that your dog will leave when asked (see Training Guide - Tug).

And also, "*My dog brings me toys and puts them on my knee. Is it*

20

okay to play with her?" Yes it is, so long as you want to play and she is asking, not telling. If you think she is telling you to play - thrusting the toy at you rather than bringing it for you - guide her into another behaviour (asking for a different toy from the toy-box is good) and reward that "Please" with the very game she wanted. Shape the behaviour into sitting beside you with the toy in her mouth - much more polite than plonking it on your knee.

Apply the principles to every activity. "Calmly sitting and looking" is good for most things, like having her lead put on, getting into/out of the car or being allowed to go play with her doggy pal in the park. You'll need to shape each one, but she'll catch on more quickly each time.

Pretty soon she'll understand that she can ask you for every activity she values by being calm and looking at you to say, "*Please*".

Now let's take the brakes off a bit. In the same way that we did with food, once she has grasped the idea you can ease your control back and allow her self-control to take over. You don't need to guide her into an extended calm-sit every time for everything. Provided she is not behaving badly she may well be being polite enough to be rewarded with any activity.

So long as what she is doing is not inappropriate you don't have to exert maximum control. That's what guidance means, allowing her to make the right decisions. She doesn't have to "do" anything to "earn" everything so long as what she is doing is appropriate. Standing still for her lead clipped on is fine; dropping the ball at your feet for another throw is fine; leaning her head on your knee and looking imploringly to be taken for a walk is fine.

The attractiveness of this light touch is that if she does start to become over-excited and you think it is appropriate just to calm her down a little, you both know how to do it.

Say, for example, she responds to your taking control with

guidance really well, has stopped barging and simply checks in as she calmly walks through any door you open for her. There is no need to keep stopping and guiding her into "calm sitting and looking" every time, because her behaviour is already appropriate. So long as she continues to do that you have a great arrangement with minimal effort.

However, if for some reason she becomes over-excited, perhaps by an increased incentive (new boyfriend outside?), you can drop back into guiding her again, but probably just for the next two or three activities until she remembers her manners.

The question is, "*Is she doing this in an appropriate mannerly way?*" If the answer is "*Yes*", then reward her with the very activity she sought. If the answer is "*No*", provide her with some guidance that re-establishes your control of the situation before she gets her reward.

Interaction

There is some overlap between activities and our final category, Interaction, because so many activities also include at least a degree of interaction with people. The people we are talking about here are those that have value for the dog, so they will be his family. Incidentally, you are not his pack; dogs chose to become part of human families, we did not choose to integrate ourselves into wolf-packs.

You do him no favours treating him like you think a dog would treat him, because he knows you aren't a dog. Dogs have evolved for twenty thousand years[2] to fit into human families, so let's not waste that. Treat him as a dog that's part of your family, with the needs of a dog, but the consideration you would expect from a family member.

The resource here is the value of the interaction with you. Dogs find interaction with people valuable. If I was to use the proper scientifically detached language, I would say that we know that dogs

---

[2] To put this in context for you, the world was in an ice-age, humans were stone-aged, and Neanderthals and mammoths still roamed Europe. Like dogs, we're still the basic package, but our manners have changed a lot since then.

value interaction with a significant attachment figure because oxytocin levels in their brain rise as a result. Less scientifically, any dog that loves you, loves interaction with you, and if he lives with you, you are his family and he loves you.

"Interaction" is anything from you; a word, a look, a touch. Unfortunately, this also includes harsh words, looks and touches. Sadly, a dog doesn't stop loving someone who abuses them, and if abuse is all they get, they can value that as interaction from a loved one. Being shouted at can be rewarding if that's all there is. Please avoid going down that rocky road.

Your dog values a word, look or touch from you, and will actively work for one. Like other resources, these forms of interaction have different values for different dogs and at different times.

It is a bit ironic that for thousands of years we have selectively bred dogs to want to be with us, dogs that love human interaction and attention, and then we complain and label them "attention-seekers".

All dogs are to some extent attention-seekers, otherwise they wouldn't bother with people at all. What we really mean when we complain about their attention-seeking behaviour is that they are interacting with us in ways that we don't find appropriate.

Some dogs can find interaction with their owner so rewarding that lack of it becomes very distressing for them. Often these dogs can be very persistent in working out strategies for controlling their owner's attention and are labelled "attention-seeking".

In order to do that, these dogs must actually believe they can control your attention. You can change that perception when you show them it is yours to give, not theirs to take.

I've left this category until last because it is the hardest one for people to practice. It is hard because it is often counter-intuitive. It is easy to see how to reward a dog's good behaviour with food, or to reward calmly sitting by opening the door (with a fanfare), and equally easy to see how the food reward can be withheld and the door not opened until you can guide the appropriate behaviour.

It is almost impossible to remove the reward of interaction from a dog that is behaving badly. You can't shout at him (that's interaction); you can't give him a "time-out" (taking him out of the room is interaction); you can't ignore him, either passively by out-waiting him, or actively by turning your back on him (remember, if Y doesn't work, he'll get Y-ier - "ignoring" can make him worse!)

So what can we do? We can guide the right behaviour before he gets it wrong. Don't wait for the wrong behaviour, but ask for the right one beforehand. Guide dogs don't wait for you to walk in front of a bus, and we shouldn't allow our pet dogs to make mistakes before guiding them.

If you are starting from scratch with a puppy or a rescue dog parachuted into his new home, you have the opportunity to take control of your interaction with him immediately. Use your words, looks and touches to reward calm behaviours. This can appear counter-intuitive because, "*He's not doing anything*" when he's being calm. But, "*Not doing anything*" is exactly what you should reward: relaxed, calm, settled behaviour.

You don't have to go overboard with lavish praise, but a quiet confirmation that he's doing the right thing will reward behaviours you want to encourage; a lingering stroke down the neck for sitting calmly, a loving glance and smile for checking in with you, "*Clever dog*" softly spoken for not rushing in.

For dogs already displaying bad manners that are being rewarded by interaction, you need to find another behaviour that can also be rewarded (preferably with interaction), and substitute that one. Dare I say that "calm sitting and looking" might fit the bill? You will need to teach it out of context, but you've probably already done that with the food and activities, so you are halfway there.

Alternatively, for behaviours where you want to reduce interaction, such as pawing or barking at you, train her to go sit on her bed in anticipation of a reward (see Training Guide - "sit-on-bed" and keep your pot of mixed food/treats handy, so you can reward her calm bed-sitting anytime you walk past).

All you need to do now is to place the new behaviour in context. The times when a dog that is behaving inappropriately (barking, jumping up, pawing) to gain access to interaction are very predictable. Your focus in changing these behaviours is in pre-empting them. Because they are predictable, this should be relatively easy, but you need to keep your eye on the ball.

Just before the unwanted behaviour would normally happen, ask for another, acceptable behaviour that you have trained out of context, and reward that with the very attention that your dog was looking for.

If it happens at a time when interaction isn't appropriate, for example dogs that bark whilst their owners are on the telephone, provide a different reward, such as a food-stuffed toy. Set up training exercises - ring your own phone so that you can train her to run to sit calmly on her bed in expectation of the treat. Or keep a loaded food-ball by the phone to use as a reward for her calmly sitting and looking at you as the phone rings, then she can play with it whilst you chat with your friends.

These alternative treats should be of very high value, because they are replacing very high value interaction, and they should always be applied by pre-empting the unwanted behaviour.

If she gets it wrong or if you don't manage to pre-empt (and we all make mistakes) simply guide her into the new behaviour, wait for a count of at least ten (beware of chaining!) and reward.

Controlling interaction is never about reducing it. She gets the same amount of interaction as she ever did - probably even more. It is about placing her behaviour initially under your control, then increasingly under her own self-control, using your interactions with her as a reward.

A word, a look or a touch is a reward. Treat them as such and be aware of what you are rewarding. Apply them onto behaviours you like and guide behaviours you don't like into better ones.

"But what about her sitting on my knee and me cuddling her because I want to? Can't I do that?" Yes, of course you can, just be aware of what she thinks got her this massive reward. So long as she thinks it was an appropriate behaviour (defined by you) that's fine. And "nothing" could be an appropriate behaviour. Cuddles for free are fine. Cuddles for tugging at your sleeve might not be.

If she leaps across the room before curling up comfortably on your lap you might want to consider guiding a more appropriate way of asking, but it isn't the comfort that is inappropriate, just the way she went about controlling it.

Ask her up for a cuddle when she's calm, or pre-empt the cross-room leap and guide a "calm sit and look" way of asking. Then invite her up for a cuddle.

Ask yourself the question, "*Whose idea was this interaction?*" If it was yours, that's fine. If it was hers, the follow-up question is, "*How did she ask?*" If the answer is, "*Very politely*" then that is fine too, so long as you want it to happen. Reward her good manners with the interaction.

If now isn't the right time, or if the behaviour is never appropriate, ask her to go sit on her bed for a little while (having trained it out of context of course) so that you can apply a reward to this appropriate behaviour a little while later.

Progress

These are big changes in your relationship, or possibly in the way that you have kept dogs before, so they may take a bit of getting your head around. But they are easy for dogs to follow because you are providing the guidance for them.

If you are starting afresh in a new relationship with a puppy or a rescue dog you will need to be very composed and think about what you are doing at every moment. What effect am I having on my dog now? Does he deserve a reward? Do I want to encourage this behaviour? What is he going to do next? Do I need to provide guidance for him?

If you are changing a current relationship with your dog, it is probably because you consider some of her behaviour to be a problem.

In that case you need to examine what you have been getting wrong in the past. You will have the benefit of being able to predict some of your dog's behaviour so that you can pre-empt and offer guidance into an alternative, but don't just concentrate on the problem; you can change your dog's whole attitude by taking control of her valued resources, which makes her much more amenable to your suggestions.

As time goes on and your relationship develops along the lines of the dog you've always wanted, you will be able to take your foot off the pedal. He will make all the right decisions by himself and won't need your guidance all the time. He'll be doing what you want him to because he wants to - it's the best way to enjoy all the things he loves in life (including you).

But don't forget to apply the rewards to his good behaviour. Take the fanfares down a bit, but keep control of the things important to him and use them to reward him whenever you can.

The human tendency is to forget him when he is behaving well - thinking he's "fixed" and doesn't need telling any more. Not so. He's behaving well because there's something in it for him - and the "something" is you - his rewarding owner. So keep up the good work, or he will look for other ways to find his rewards.

Guidance is like that; you dip in and out of it to help him when he needs it. It isn't locked-down all-out control all the time, but a light hand on the tiller to make sure that if he drifts off course a little you can easily steer his behaviour back in the right direction.

Once you get the hang of Guide & Control, dog owning becomes so much simpler. He hangs on your every word because your value is so high; training becomes easier because he wants to please you; bad manners and inappropriate behaviours disappear because there's nothing in it for him. He's a fun dog and a pleasure to own.

The next part of this booklet is a Training Guide for Sit-on-Bed, Retrieve and Tug. They can be trained in other ways, but the methods used here follow the Guide & Control principles. If you train your dog like this you will find it easier to get into the frame of mind most conducive to guiding and controlling your dog. Give it a go.

The end of the booklet summarises the important principles to help you develop your own strategies for guiding and controlling the aspects of your dog's behaviour that are most important to you, and to him.

I would say, *"Good luck"*, but you don't need luck. You need consistency, a modicum of understanding, a little bit of determination and a touch of concentration, and through guiding and controlling you will end up with the best relationship you can have with your dog.

Training Guide

Treats

Guiding and rewarding your dog teaches him quickly and efficiently. Activity and Interaction rewards come from you and your control of the environment, but using food treats can be good for training specific behaviours that aren't inherently rewarding, such as the "sit-on-bed".

First you will need to manage a supply of treats. They should be very high value for your dog, so maybe little pieces of cheese or cooked meat. Commercial treats are okay if your dog likes them. They should be very small so he gets a taste, but doesn't fill up with junk food; about the size of your little fingernail for a Labrador-sized dog.

Because you are adding treats you should consider his diet generally. Most commercial dog foods supply all the nutritional needs for most dogs, so if you are using a good quality one of them, that's great, but if we add too many treats we will upset the balance.

A good way to control the amount of treats he has throughout the day is to weigh out his daily ration of dog-food into his bowl first thing. If it is a complete diet of dried kibble, that's fine; if it is a meat and biscuit combo, don't add the meat at this stage.

Take a little of the kibble away and mix in the same bulk of treats - no more than 5% (20th). You now have a treat/food mix to reward him with throughout the day.

When you want to reward him, don't look in the bowl, but dip in randomly and use the first piece that comes to hand. That way, your rewards will be different - and he won't know when it is a little reward (kibble) or a big one (cheese). Randomising rewards like this has been shown to actually increase the effort dogs put in to working for them.

If your dog has more than one meal each day, transfer the portion of his food to another bowl for the first meals, fishing out the treats, and the final meal is whatever is left in the daily allowance. This allows you to treat, but not over-feed him. If you are adding dog-meat to biscuits, do that just before you feed him.

If you like to share your own food with your dog (and many owners do) make sure that it isn't harmful. Check with your vet if in any doubt, but avoid grapes, raisins and chocolate (a fruit and nut bar is a definite no-no).

Rather than feeding him from your own plate, pop your left-overs or shares in his food-bowl and save them for his last meal of the day (by the way, this counts as part of his treat allocation, not in addition to it). You get to share, he gets the enjoyment, and you avoid a drooling, begging dog around the table.

You've now got a bowl (or plastic box with snap-on lid) of food and treats to dip into throughout the day to reward any behaviour you like.

Sit on Bed

Training your dog to "sit-on-bed" is a relatively simple process, but you can make it easier if you treat it as a training exercise, rather than letting it evolve over time.

You will find it really helpful if you can keep his daily food/treat bowl on a shelf above his bed - or at least nearby and high enough that he can't reach it. If you can't (for example in warm weather), try a smaller treat-pot with just a proportion of mixed food and treats in it.

Take a small tasty treat from the ration and show it to him to start with. Lure him with the treat in your hand by walking over to the bed, saying, "*On your bed*" in an encouraging tone. It's not a punishment, so keep your voice really friendly.

When he stands on the bed, take your hand over his head so that his nose reaches back and his bum goes down. The minute his bum hits the bed, reward with the treat. Now let him see you reach into the food/treat bowl you cunningly placed above his bed, and reward him again with a random treat.

As you walk away, he will probably come with you. After a few steps, turn around and say, "*On your bed*" again, making the same luring motion with your hand, although there is nothing in it. When he is again on the bed, tip his head up and his bum down with the same motion as before and, when his bum hits the bed, reach up into the bowl and take a reward for him.

He is getting the idea that if he goes to his bed you will reward him from the conveniently situated stash of treats. Now you don't have to bribe him by showing him a treat before he will sit on his bed because he knows that the treats are waiting there for him.

Repeat the training for five or six trials before finishing with a reward, then leave it an hour or two before giving it another go.

Once he has the idea, you can extend the amount of time he sits there before treating him; a few seconds, then a few more. You can also occasionally (once a day?) provide a big treat in the form of a chew or stuffed food-toy to eat on his bed whilst he relaxes there.

As you move around the house during the day, occasionally send him off to his bed, so he learns to go from anywhere. You will need to follow him and, because he has scampered there quicker than you, he will sit and wait for you to arrive, extending the time before you reward him of his own accord.

Once he has the idea, you don't have to reward him with a food-treat every time (although you should still tell him he has been a good dog), but he will continue to go there for the possibility of a treat every time. Like varying the quality of the treat, varying the frequency also makes him keener.

Basically you are making going to and staying on his bed a pleasant experience, so you can use it to pre-empt and guide him away from other behaviours. Rather than saying, *"Don't do that"* you can predict or interrupt inappropriate behaviours by asking him to go to his bed instead, controlling, guiding and rewarding him.

Games

There are two main games in which owners interact with their pet dogs: the retrieve and the tug. Keeping them under control ensures maximum enjoyment and allows you to use them to guide your dog's other behaviour. This is how:

Retrieve

Because this is a teaching exercise you should start in a place with few distractions so your dog is able to learn more quickly. Sitting on the floor with her in the living room, without any other dogs, cats or children to get in the way is good.

The toy should be something that she really likes, easy to pick up and big enough so that it won't jam in her throat. For ease of explanation I'm going to use a ball.

I prefer not to use a squeaky for a retrieve toy because it encourages chewing (to make it squeak) and the enjoyment is supposed to be in the interaction, not in going off by herself to enjoy the squeaky noise. If you want to give her a squeaky toy to play with by herself, that's fine, so long as you know the reason she likes it is that it simulates a small dying animal that she is chomping on, which encourages her to destroy it even more.

Buy two identical balls. In fact, if they are in a sale, buy loads, because you may well lose a few and there's nothing quite as bad as losing her favourite ball and not having a replacement to hand.

Sit with her and get her attention by rolling the ball around on the floor in front of her, or bouncing it gently. When she's following it around the floor in your hand, roll it away from you past her nose so she chases and picks it up.

Now ignore her and play with the other ball on the floor by yourself. The one she has hold of has value for her, so why should she give it back to you? She needs a reason to do that, and you provide that reason by showing that the one you have is more exciting than the one she has. That's the purpose of having two.

Some dogs will run over and drop the first ball in order to play with the second one the instant you show it to them. Others will need a little persuading. You can do that in various ways, for example by rolling it from one hand to the other, bouncing or tossing it in

the air, or making feints at throwing it. For really resistant dogs you can conceal a squeaky (from a toy she has already destroyed) in your hand and squeeze it to make the noise as you play with the ball.

When she runs over and drops the first ball because she wants the second, reward her by rolling away the second ball (do not let go of the squeaky - only the ball in your hand squeaks). Now you have the first ball again and can repeat the procedure.

Shape your result by increasing or decreasing the attraction of the ball you have compared to the one she has. If she drops it too soon, hide your ball behind your back and encourage her to go back for hers.

Manipulate what she does by changing what you do. You can also shape her dropping it into your hand if you like.

Pretty soon she will be chasing a ball and bringing it back to exchange for the one she knows you have. At that point you can keep the other ball in your pocket and make a show of bringing it out to exchange.

Now you don't need the sight of the other ball; simply putting your hand in your pocket will be enough to make her drop the ball she has, as she expects you to produce the other. This is the point at which you can introduce a cue word. Say, "*Drop*", "*Leave*" (or "*Cheesecake ice-cream*" - it doesn't matter so long as you are consistent) just before you plunge your hand theatrically into your pocket. The word predicts that something good is about to appear so she might as well give up what she has, NOT that you're about to take something from her.

You can choose to either reward with the ball in your pocket, or to pick up and throw the one she has just dropped. Once she has the basic idea, you can factor in all sorts of modifications, for example, use different toys, or change locations, then take the game out on walks and introduce your ball-chucking stick. Because the retrieve game is now such fun it has great value for her and you can use it as a reward for any behaviour you like when out and about.

A slight word of warning for obsessive types (the dogs that is, not you) - don't overdo the game to the extent that she does nothing else on walks - calmer behaviours like sniffing about and meeting friends are important too.

To make sure that she knows when the offer of the game is over, place the ball in your pocket and give a clear, "*Finished*" signal, both verbally and by showing her your empty hands.

Tug

Yes, there are some dogs that shouldn't play rough competitive games and these especially include those that haven't learned to inhibit their biting. You will know if you have one of these because you will also have bruises and possibly deeper wounds.

The other type of dog is one that is physically stronger than their owner and does not self-handicap, so that the game comprises of the dog pulling the owner over. You will know if you have one of these from the graze marks on your nose and knees from being dragged across the floor.

In both these cases the game is so unpleasant for the owner that they have usually already decided not to play.

However, the majority of dogs can play tug provided they are taught not to be too rough, and it is in teaching that level of moderation where a little skill comes in.

First choose your tug toy, then buy two (or more if in a sale). The traditional rope type is fine, but it needs to be longer than the width of your dog's mouth and both your hands. If you are keen on a one-handed rubber type, might need to alter your strategy a little (see later).

The customary method of waving the toy in the general direction of your dog's mouth to encourage him to grab at it usually results in just that. You are now holding one end and your dog has the other. Pulling towards you should encourage your dog to pull back, possibly growling. This isn't anything to worry about, so long as it remains in play.

Play the tug game for a few minutes, allowing him to win some ground occasionally but not to drag you round the room. You should aim for a 50/50 split of winning and losing for most fun.

If he gets too competitive and you need to take the game down a little, stop pulling. I appreciate this will be slightly difficult as he will continue to pull, but you need to make the game no fun.

Take hold of the rope tug in both hands, one at each side of his head, and turn it so that it is vertical; one end pointing at your foot and the other upwards. Then pull it tightly against your leg and lock it out. If you can't pull the tug to the leg, take the leg to the tug. Locking it against your leg like this provides you with greater stability.

If you can get this right (practice without a dog) there should be little or no give in the rope. The vertical rope makes it uncomfortable for him to pull, holding his head sideways, and as he will not be able to move it at all, he will soon give up - it's no fun.

To prevent him going in for the bite again as soon as you move the rope, keep it against your leg, straighten up and take it immediately behind your back. Then ask him to sit as you slowly bring the rope back around the front. If he moves towards the rope at all raise it above his jumping height. Like we did with the food bowl, if he stays calm the rope comes back, but if he doesn't it goes away again.

If he doesn't give up when you lock the rope out, or if your full reach is not high enough to keep it above his jumping height, consider if you really should be playing tug with him, before you get the grazes.

Keep him sitting calmly for a few seconds, then reward him with the very thing he wanted, the rope waved in his face for a renewed game. Play again, keeping him within the moderate play-zone. If he tips towards over-excited, lock the rope out against your leg again. When he leaves it ask for sit and calm, then reward again.

Judging the point at which it is fun but not too manic is the key. Keep the game sufficiently well-mannered by removing the fun when he goes too far, then bringing it back conditional on a little bit of calm.

Reward the exact behaviour you want from him. You can put a nice friendly "*Leave*" request when you lock the rope out, but don't repeat it.

Soon you should have a nice virtuous cycle of a fun tug game regularly punctuated by him leaving the rope then asking politely for another tug.

Should he be allowed to win it altogether? Yes, he can from time to time, but that's when you produce the second rope from your pocket and play with it by yourself (see the Retrieve training for the logic). Your rope is fun, but his is less fun.

Always finish by taking possession of both ropes and asking him for calm. Use a "*Finished*" as in the Retrieve and put the ropes out of reach.

If you have a tug-toy that is not suitable for locking out against your leg, you might look at other options, such as pulling it in to your body as tightly as you can, for no-give stability, and/or exchanging it for another, produced as something more exciting.

Both Tug and Retrieve

There are other ways to teach your pet to give up toys when asked and provided they are safe and work by enhancing your relationship (not by risking it) there is no harm in them.

For example, food treats can be used to exchange for toys so long as you beware of chaining. Dogs have been known to "steal" or keep hold of toys in order to make their owner stump-up a treat.

No matter what method you use, you can always provide a small food treat when the game is over, so it is not a total loss when the toy goes away. Use the "*Finished*" to signal a treat arriving as the game ends.

There is no need for your pet dog to be calamitously giddy when playing games. Of course you *should* play games with your dog, but on your terms, not solely his. Controlling the way he plays allows him the fun, whilst keeping it pleasurable for you too. It also keeps your personal value very high (because you are access to fun), reduces conflict between you because the competition remains play (not real) and gives him an appropriate way of using up some energy, with manners.

Summary

Controlling resources

Resources are the things your dog values.

Control the resource and you control the dog:

Food

Food belongs to you. You bought it; you own it - even dog-food. If your dog would like access to any food, she must either ask nicely, with a good-mannered way of saying "please", as you offer it, or simply to behave in a way you would like to reward.

Activities

Your dog enjoys many activities. It is good manners for her to ask permission from you to partake in any of them. It also increases your value because you are access to fun! For access to even the simplest activity your dog should be calm. Initially you may need to encourage calm by asking for a "sit" or a "sit and look". The reward is being allowed to enjoy the activity, whether it is a sniff around the garden or getting into the car to go for a play with the dogs in the park.

Interaction

You are probably the resource your dog values most. You belong to you. You are not here to be manipulated by your dog. Interaction is a touch, a look or a word from you. Use them as you would use a treat-reward, because that's how your dog views them. Apply them selectively on behaviours you like - especially when your dog is calm of her own accord. It is okay to interact for free, so long as your dog is not doing anything inappropriate that she could mistakenly think prompted you to reward her.

Pre-empt - Guide - Reward

Guide good behaviour using preferred resources as rewards:

Pre-empt - Pay attention to your dog. If she's "not doing anything" she's probably being good. Tell her, and sometimes reward her. You will soon be able to predict when she is about to drop into inappropriate behaviours. That means that you can intervene before she starts and avoid reinforcing inappropriate behaviour with an interaction.

Guide - Before your dog makes a mistake, guide an alternative, preferable behaviour. In many cases this might just be checking in with you. Don't let her walk into the lamppost; guide her around it. Use her trained behaviours to provide alternatives if you need to.

Reward - When she gets it right, use one of her favourite resources (food, activity or interaction) as a reward. If you can, reward with the resource she was aiming for in the first place; if you can't, provide a higher value alternative.

Oops! - If you make a mistake and she drops into an inappropriate behaviour, guide her into a better alternative that you can reward. Make sure you leave time between the two to prevent chaining the behaviours together.

Progress - Over time you will be able to lighten your touch to monitoring and providing occasional guidance, as your dog starts to exert self-control. Of course you can always re-apply Guide & Control to a greater or lesser extent if you need to later.

Finally - Always apply resource-rewards to your dog's good behaviour. It is polite for her to say, "*Please*" but equally polite for you to say, "*Thank you*".

Other books by David Ryan

Dog Secrets - Ironically titled because there are no "secrets", just things you haven't yet learned, this is a common-sense training book about understanding dogs and teaching methods that work.

"*Stop!*" How to control predatory chasing in dogs - looks at the reasons for inappropriate predatory chasing, the more effective solutions and how to go about changing the behaviour.

Dogs that Bite and Fight - provides a complete understanding of why pet dogs bite and fight, how to prevent it and how to change the behaviour, including training methods that owners can use with their own pets.

Available from good bookshops (on and off-line) and through David's website http://www.dog-secrets.co.uk in hard copy and e-formats to suit all readers.